A. R. Edwards
PHOTOGRAPHIC ARCHIVE

*Covering their hometown of Selkirk
and The Borders*

Compiled by
Janis Cornwall

•

A Selkirk Regeneration Company project
A Limited Company Registered in Scotland. No. SC365167
Registered Office:
Woodlands, 46 Hillside Terrace, Selkirk TD7 4ND
Registered Charity No. SCO37397

A. R. Edwards
Photographic Archive
1879 - 1965

Covering their hometown of Selkirk
and The Borders

First published June 2017 by dbethune.com
Contents © Selkirk Regeneration Company

ISBN 978-0-9576779-3-7

Printed by
Bordersprint Ltd., 2-4 West Port, Selkirk TD7 4DG

A. R. Edwards
Photographic Archive

*Covering their hometown of Selkirk
and The Borders*

*"Old Photographers never die...
They just go out of focus"*

To the best of our knowledge all photographs in this book
are the work of A. R. Edwards. If we have included any
that are not, our apologies for any inconvenience caused.

*Dr. Lindsay Neil
Selkirk Regeneration Company*

Contents

Foreword

It is not given to many of us nowadays to open an undiscovered window into the past. Howard Carter's pulse must have raced and he must have felt privileged and amazed when he first saw into Tutankhamun's tomb, its contents unseen and hidden for millennia. "Wonderful things…" he said.

So it was, on a much smaller scale, when we first saw the collection of photographs taken by the Edwards dynasty in Selkirk but it was no less impressive.

From his first arrival in the Borders, Andrew Edwards, succeeded by his son Robert and granddaughter Bessie, faithfully recorded Border scenes, people and events continuously from 1879 to the early 1960s.

Nearly all the studio photographs have not survived so we are not encumbered with identifying endless mystery people. What has survived, thanks to Bessie and her daughter Cathy is an archive of instantly recognisable Border places in both town and country and the fascinating record of how things have changed (and remained the same) during the last nearly 140 years.

This book is a collation of the most interesting and largely unpublished photographs taken by the Edwards family. They show what the Borders was like before and just after the advent of the motor car. Some buildings are gone but are recorded at the pinnacle of their grandeur before dilapidation, infestations and impoverishment dictated their demolition.

The Selkirk Regeneration Company has taken on the task of consolidating the scattered collection, recording these images of the Borders past and making them accessible to all in book form. A Scottish Borders Council grant has made the publication possible and we are grateful for their support.

Immense tribute is due to Janis Cornwall for her tireless editing of the images, hiding defects and unwanted lettering, her deleting of cracks in glass negatives and general enhancement of the older pictures. She has spent many hours at it resulting in a very professional outcome cooperating at every stage with the printers, James and Cath Rutherford of Bordersprint in Selkirk.

Selkirk photographs are in the majority but as the Edwards went all round the Borders taking pictures, there are old photographs of most of the Borders towns and villages as well, not just Selkirk.

Dr Lindsay Neil
Selkirk Regeneration Company

A. R. EDWARDS & SON
Photographers • Selkirk
1879 -1965

Andrew Robert Edwards was born on 30th December 1847 in Badminton, near Chipping Sodbury. He was the son of Agnes Edwards (neé Campbell) and Mathew Edwards, soldier (as written on his birth certificate.)

Andrew grew up and found his way to Scotland where he was employed by Messrs Blackwood & Co., Publishers, Edinburgh, as a compositor. Showing a great interest in the fine art of photography, Andrew moved on to Aberdeen where he was engaged by the famous George Washington Wilson Photographic Company.

After several years working for GWW, and gaining much experience and knowledge of photography, Andrew aspired to setup business on his own. By this time, Andrew had met and married Jane Plant and they were living at 21 Henry Street, Aberdeen. Andrew and Jane's first-born son Robert arrived on 9th November 1877 and some two years later, the family prepared to move south to Selkirk.

In February 1879, the local press featured a short article entitled:-

NEW PHOTOGRAPHIC STUDIO

"A.R. Edwards begs to inform the Gentry and Public generally of Selkirk and neighbourhood that he will shortly open a new PHOTOGRAPHIC STUDIO at Myrtle Bank, Tower Street for the production of Portraits of all styles. Mr. Edwards has acquired the newest and best appliances for producing Good Artistic Portraits, and begs particularly, to draw attention to his New Baby Lens which enables him to take instantaneous portraits, so invaluable in the case of children.

Having had many years of experience, and been for the last four years with Messers G.W.Wilson & Co of Aberdeen, he hopes to be able to execute all orders to the satisfaction of his customers.

Till the erection of his Studio is finished, Mr. Edwards will be happy to undertake all out-door work – such as Photographing Views, Gentleman's Seats, Interiors of Churches, Drawing-Rooms &c.; likewise Horses, Cattle, &c." *Aberdeen, 25th Feb 1879.*

Andrew's attempts to open a studio in Selkirk had a few setbacks and he wrote a short intimation in the local press, quote:-

"Mr. A.R. Edwards, photographer, apologises to the public for the delay in opening his Studio. The progress of its erection has been much hindered by unfavourable weather and some time must yet elapse before it is fully completed. He regrets the unavoidable delay and bespeaks the further forbearance of those who have arranged for sittings, for a little longer. Due notice of opening, will of course be given." *Tower Street, May 7th, 1879.*

Later that year another short article appeared in the local press which read:-

NEW PHOTOGRAPHIC STUDIO

"A.R. Edwards has pleasure in intimating to the inhabitants of Selkirk and District that he is now prepared to take Portraits in all Styles and Sizes. Children are taken instantaneously, and parties are desired to bring them between the hours of Eleven and One o'clock. For the convenience of all parties it is desirable that engagements be made beforehand."

Single Cards 7s and Groups 8s per Dozen.
Highly Finished (Modeled), 10s per Dozen

A.R. Edwards, Tower Street, Selkirk

So Andrew was finally in business! His second son John had been born and was four months old. John was born in Dalmeny, West Lothian, presumably Andrews wife Jane, went to a member of the family to give birth as Andrew would have been away from Aberdeen overseeing the works on his studio in Selkirk.

Andrew was an ambitious man and was already thinking of a second studio, and in 1882 he opened in The Bongate Jedburgh. This branch was open for nine years closing

DEATH OF MR A. R. EDWARDS.—This well-known member of the community of Selkirk died yesterday afternoon. Mr Edwards had not been in good health for some time, but it was only within the past fortnight that serious apprehensions began to be entertained as to his condition. He was able to be out of doors on Monday, and spent a little while in the garden ; but from that time he got gradually worse and sank rapidly. Mr Edwards began life as a compositor in the printing office of Messrs Blackwood and Co., publishers, Edinburgh. Before completing his apprenticeship, he manifested a decided liking and fine taste for the photographic art, and readily obtained employment from the firm of Messrs G. W. Wilson & Co., Aberdeen. He had a fine eye for the selection of scenic subjects, and a large number of the firm's earlier series of views of Scottish scenery were Mr Edwards' productions. He had thus visited most of the famous parts of Scotland. His first acquaintance with Selkirk was made when on a tour in the Border district for Messrs Wilson, and not long afterwards he commenced business in the town, now about twelve years ago. Mr Edwards opened a branch studio in Jedburgh, and there, as in Selkirk, his services were much in request by all classes. Deceased was a man of mild manners and quiet disposition, and sought retirement rather than prominence as a citizen. He had, however, well-formed opinions on public questions. For some years he was treasurer of the Selkirk Liberal Association, and he took a warm interest in the cause of the men in the late railway strike. It was indeed principally through his exertions that the public meeting was got up in the town, and that subscriptions to the amount of £26 were raised in behalf of the strike fund. Mr Edwards leaves a widow and four of a family.

in 1891 when Andrew died at the early age of forty two from a heart condition.

Andrew was survived by his wife Jane, his two sons Robert and John, and two daughters Helen and Agnes.

Robert had amassed a considerable portfolio of photographs, postcard views, portraits and cartes de visite. There were also a significant amount of glass plate negatives, a few of which have survived today.

Some years before he died, Andrew had employed a young assistant by the name of Thomas Hughs Milner Colledge. Thomas proved to be a very competent photographer and took over the A R Edwards business until Andrew's eldest son Robert was of age to take up the reigns.

Mr. Colledge also established a successful photographic business of his own in Innerleithen which operated from 1893 to1914.

ROBERT EDWARDS
b.1877- d.1965

Robert Edwards was only about twelve years old when his father Andrew died but having grown up within a photographic family, Robert had some knowledge of the art. Even at this early age, Robert could have learnt much from his father about photography, subsequently, by the time Robert was twenty, he was a fully-fledged photographer well able to run the family business.

(It is thought that Robert did engage in some formal training in Photography but it is not known where.)

Robert had some very distinguished clients and photographed royalty when they visited local notable estates. In 1923 two letters of appreciation arrived from the then Duke and Duchess of York thanking Robert for his excellent photographs taken on their visits to Abbotsford House and Eildon Hall. One letter was sent from H M Yacht Victoria and Albert, and another from White Lodge Richmond Park bearing the duke of Yorks Crest. A third letter of appreciation dated 1935 (bearing a black border), was sent on the occasion of the Duke of Buccleuch's death. Robert had sent his condolences and two photographs to the Dukes widow the Duchess of Gloucester.

These letters must have been of great significance and prestige to Robert and his business.

Robert concentrated on portraiture work in the daylight studio and many families and children came to have their photos taken.

Otherwise Robert concentrated on landscape views which were used for postcards, but some of his best landscapes he enlarged and framed. These were hung in the reception room at the studio at 73 Tower Street.

Robert entered two photographs in the 1900 Edinburgh Photographic Society's annual exhibition, one a portrait of a dog and another a detailed image of a daisy. For these two exhibits, Robert was awarded two medals, which demonstrates his work was held in high regard.

Using glass plate processing, Robert took meticulous care to touch up negatives to eliminate any flaws in the glass-plate image. Touching up involved putting the negative on an easel with a gap in the middle and a light bulb behind it .The negative was then placed in front of the gap so the light shining through it would show up any flaws in the negative. Robert would then work with a tiny paintbrush and black pigment, to paint over any spots where the light shone through erroneously.

As a member of the Selkirk Bowling club, Robert was a keen player and won matches quite frequently over the years. He was also a member of the Selkirk Antiquarian Society and he took an active interest in local history. Signing the pledge of the 'Christian Temperance Campaign' in 1910, Robert was tee-total all his life. "I hereby promise, by the help of God, to abstain from all intoxicating Liquors as beverages". The temperance movement had a strong following at this time.

Married on 25th July 1908 to Margaret Johnston Reid Aitchison, of Edinburgh, Robert settled into life as a family man. Margaret – or Peggy as she was known – gave birth to three children to Robert, the eldest Bert, then Bessie, then Jack.

All the children were involved in the business in some capacity at some point in their lives. Bessie left Selkirk in the early 1940s to study

photography in London at the Bloomsbury Technical College for Ladies.

With the innovation of simpler photographic techniques by the early 1960s, Robert decided it was time to consider retirement. He was now in his mid-eighties and over the next few years the business was wound down and the studio sold.

Robert was, however, still a very active man and he remained so until his sudden death whilst on holiday in Dunbar on the 4th June 1965 at the age of eighty-seven.

It was the end of an era for A. R. Edwards and Son.

Bessie continued to have an interest in photography and preserved and looked after much of the accumulated negatives, some on glass, which show vignettes of the local scenes and events from the early times until the 1960s.

Subsequently, Cathy Chick, A. R. Edwards' great-granddaughter and Bessie's daughter, entrusted this unique collection of images to the Selkirk Regeneration Company, the members of which, with a grant from Scottish Borders Council, set about restoring the archive. This involved repairing some damage and tracking down image details before the final production of this book of photographs, many of which had lain hidden for more than 100 years.

Selkirk

◀ *The Stane Brig, Selkirk*   ▲ *Pant Well, Selkirk Market Place*

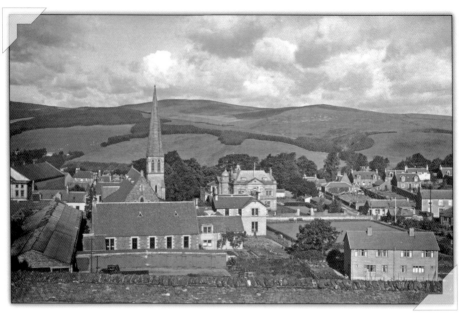

▲*Beechbank*　　　　　　　　　　▼ *St. Boswells Road*

16

▲ *Selkirk Bowling Green*   ▼ *St. Boswells Road*

Unveiling of the Flodden Memorial, Victoria Halls, Selkirk, 1913

▲ *Ettrick Water c1917*　　　　　　　▼ *Bridge Street, Selkirk*

▲*County Buildings*

▼ *The Burgh School, 1900*

▲▼ *Two views of Charabancs in Selkirk Market Square*

▲ *County Hotel*　　　　　　　　　　　▼ *High Street, 1950s*

▲ *View from Woodburn*   ▼ *Curror Street*

▲ *View from Selkirk Golf Course* ▼ *Looking to Selkirk Hills*

▲ *View from Selkirk Golf Course*　　　　　▼ *From Greenhead*

25

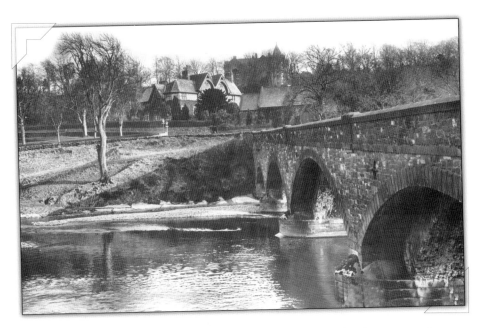

▲ *The Stane Brig, Selkirk*   ▼ *The Glen Hotel*

▲ *Sheep crossing the Stane Brig*   ▼ *Selkirk Cauld, 1936*

▲ Robert Edwards at Selkirk Bowling Club, 1960s   ▼ High Street, Park Monument

▲ *Mungo Park Monument and the Back Row*   ▼ *High Street*

▲ *Hill Street*   ▼ *Marion Crescent*

▲ *An unidentified building in Selkirk Market Place acting in part as premises for "Lees Upholsterer". Laurie, Iron & Seed Merchants is on far left.*

▼ *West Port from Market Place*

▲ *View along Tower Street to Peat Law beyond*   ▼ *Market Place*

▲▼ *Two views of Selkirk Market Place looking towards the High Street*

▲ *Selkirk Market Place, 1960s*

▼ *Market Place, early 1900s*

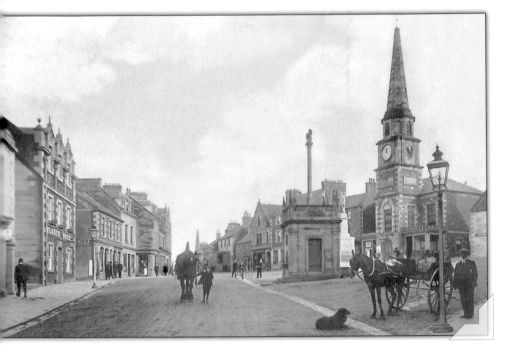

▲▼ *Two views of Selkirk Market Place*

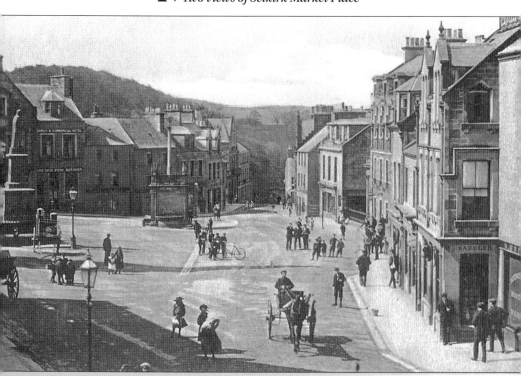

▲ ▼ *Two views of the Old Brig Road*

▲ *Old Brig Road*　　　　　　　　　▼ *Selkirk from Shawmount*

◄ *Selkirk War Memorial*

► *The former French prisoners' café, established during the Napoleonic war in Selkirk Market Place*

Selkirk Jail ▶

▼
*St John's
Church in
winter*

▲ *Selkirk from the Northwest, 1906*　　　　　　▼*Heatherlie*

▲ *Selkirk from Woodburn*   ▼ *A view down Forest Road from the County buildings*

▲ *Selkirk from the Northwest*

▲▼ *Three views of the Old West Church, Selkirk, now demolished*

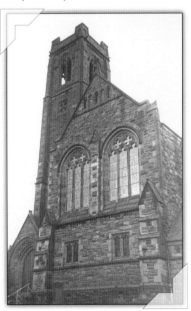

► *The Flodden Memorial, Scott's Place*

▼ *The Victoria Halls, with the Flodden Memorial just visible in front, and the Lawson Memorial Church*

▲▼ Changing times - motorised transport and covered carts in Selkirk Market Place

▲▼ Motorised vehicles take the place of horse and cart in Selkirk West Port

▲▼ *Two views of The Green from the Haining Gates, down and up.*

▲▼ *Looking down West Port... and up it to Market Place*

49

▲▼ *Tower Street, from the bottom… and the top*

▲ *The Glebe, Selkirk*   ▼ *Westfield, 86 Forest Road, Selkirk*

▲ *View over Selkirk from Manor Hill*   ▼ *Shawmount Farm 1947 (by Bessie Chick)*

The Haining Estate

▲ *View from Haining House to lakeside walk*   ▼ *Haining House*

▲ Half-way round lakeside walk   *▼ Haining House from Drive*

▲ *Two views of Haining House from lakeside walk*

▲ *Royal Company of Archers, 1930*   ▼ *Hunt meet at the Haining Gates*

▶
*The Lady's Walk
at the Haining*

◀ *Haining House
and lakeside walk*

▲▼ *Camp of the Lothians and Borders Horse, May 1915, Chicken Acre, Haining*

▲▼ *Two views of Haining Loch from the southernmost stretch of the walk*

▲ *Postcard pictures of Haining House, summer and winter*

▲ *Two views of Haining House from lakeside walk. The building to the left of the House in the top photograph was destroyed by fire in 1944*

Selkirk Common Riding

Mr. G. E. Roberts, Standard-Bearer
Selkirk Common–Riding. 1938.

Selkirk Common–Riding, 1904.

MR WILLIAM IRVINE,
STANDARD-BEARER.

These Royal Burgh Standard Bearers of 1904, 1905 and 1938 are just three of the scores of Common Riding Principals captured by the cameras of A.R. Edwards, Photographers

▲ *Bussin' the Colours*   ▼ *Doon the Green*

▲ *Gathering in the Market Place*   ▼ *Doon the Green with the Silver Band*

▲▼ Crowds move down Mill Street on the way to the river crossing

▲ ▼*Riders cross the River Ettrick*

▼◀▲
Riders stop at the Linglie for the traditional
rum-and-milk refreshment before heading up to
the Three Brethren and on round the Marches

▲ *Coming in at the toll*   ▼ *Riders gather at the toll*

▲▼ Crowds on the toll banking to cheer those returning from riding the Marches

▲▼ *The toll banking crowds welcome back the cavalcade of riders*

▲ *Townsfolk, horsemen, musicians and Craftsmen move along Scott's Place to the Casting*

*▼◄ Revellers, riders, the
Silver Band and members
of the Crafts pass along
Scott's Place to the
Casting of the Colours in
the Market Place*

*▲ The Casting of the Colours
in Selkirk Market Place*

The Casting of the Colours in Selkirk Market Place

Ettrick Valley

Oakwood Tower, now Aikwood Tower

Cottages at Oakwood

▲ *Kirkhope Tower*

▼ *Ettrick Water from Howden*

79

▲ *Colin's Bridge, Bowhill*　　　　　　　　▼ *Ettrick Bridge*

Ettrickbridge

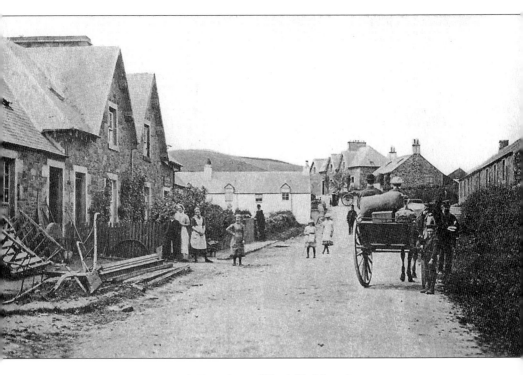

▲ *Two views of Ettrickbridgend*

▲ *Brockhill Bridge, Ettrickbridge*   ▼ *Ettrickbridge from Redhill*

▲ *Two views of Ettrickshaws House and Pine Lodge*

▲ *Cacrabank, Ettrick, and Rankle Burn*

▼ *Harvest Stooks, Ettrick*

▶
Harvest time,
Ettrick Valley

Bowhill

▲ *Bowhill House*

◣
Bridge on the Bowhill walk

▶
Newark School,
Bowhill Estate

Newark Tower, Yarrow

▲▼ Two views of Newark Tower and Yarrow Water

Yarrow Valley

*Yarrowford
in summer*

▲ *Foulshiels, Yarrow, the birthplace of African explorer Mungo Park*

▼ *Broadmeadows, Yarrow*

▲ *Hangingshaw Cottages* ▼ *Hangingshaw, Yarrow*

▲ *Two views of Yarrow Parish Kirk*

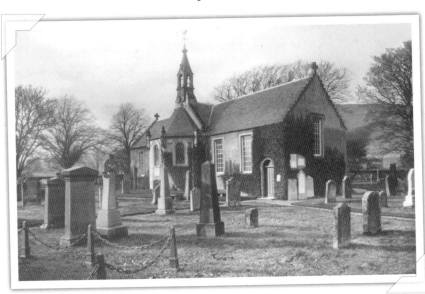

▲ *Deuchar Bridge, Yarrow*   ▼ *Yarrow Kirk*

▲ *Eldinhope, Yarrow, formerly 'Altrieve' and home of James Hogg, the Ettrick Shepherd, after it was gifted to him rent free in 1815 by the Duke of Buccleuch*

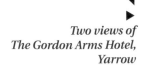

Two views of The Gordon Arms Hotel, Yarrow

St Mary's Loch, Tibbie's and Megget views

▶▼

Two views of Tibbie Shiels and St Mary's Loch, with the Loch of the Lowes beyond

▲ *St Mary's Loch* ▼ *The Rodono Hotel overlooking St Mary's Loch*

▲ Bridge at Tibbie's ▼ Tibbie's, with St Mary's Loch on left and Loch of the Lowes, right

*Writer and Ettrick
shepherd James Hogg's
statue overlooking
St Mary's Loch*

▼ *Walking beside
St Mary's Loch*

▲▼◢ *Three views of Tibbie Shiels Inn with various structural additions alongside*

▲ *Tibbie Shiels with her son Willie outside the Inn*

► *Visitors to Tibbie's travel in open carriages down the Devil's Elbow*

◄ *Tibbie Shiels, landlady of the Inn at St Mary's Loch/ Loch o'The Lowes*

▼ *Tibbie Shiels' kitchen and box bed*

▲ *Bridge over Megget Water, St Mary's Loch*   ▼ *Megget, now the location of a reservoir*

Philiphaugh

▲ *Philiphaugh. 1933*   ▼ *The Damside walk at Philiphaugh*

▲ *The Meeting of the Ettrick and Yarrow Waters at Philiphaugh*

▲ *Conservatory at Philiphaugh House*

▼*Scottish Automobile rally at Philiphaugh, 1931*

Yair

▲ *The Yair*

◥ *Yair Brig*

▶

Fishing the Tweed at Yair

▲ *The Yair*　　　　　　　　　▼ *View from Yair Bridge*

Lindean and Sunderland Hall

Sunderland Hall

▲ *Sunderland Hall*　　　　　　　　　▼ *Meeting of Ettrick and Tweed*

▲▼ *Two views of Sunderland Hall*

▼ *The Ettrick from Lindean Bridge*　▲ *Tweed Bridge from the demolished railway bridge*

◄ *View along the road from Lindean to Bridgelands*

Midlem, Lilliesleaf and Bowden

◀▲

*Two
views of
Midlem
village*

120

▲ *Free range hens at Midlem*　　　　▼ *Midlem village, spring 1931*

▲ *A postman delivers mail to Midlem village*

▼ *Midlem from east*

▲ *Midlem looking south*　　　▼ *Maxpoffle and the Eildons from Bowden*

123

▲▼ *Two views of Lilliesleaf*

124

▲ *Riddell,*
Lilliesleaf, now
demolished
                    ▶

    Lilliesleaf west

▼ *Cavers Carre*
House, Lilliesleaf

▲ *The birthplace of Thomas Aird, Bowden*　　▼ *The Fountain at Bowden village*

St Boswells, Mertoun, Eildon, Bemersyde, and Dryburgh

*◄▲ St Boswells
and villager
with donkey*

▲ *Looking across Mertoun Bridge, St. Boswells*   ▼ *The Hunt at St. Boswells*

▶ *Brae Heads, St. Boswells*

▼ *Mertoun Bridge*

▲ *Mertoun, St Boswells*　　　　　▼ *The Eildons from St Boswells*

▲▼ *Two views of the Dryburgh Abbey Hotel, St Boswells*

▲ *Eildon Hall*

▼ *Scott's view*

▲ *Scott's view*   ▼ *Royalty at Eildon Hall, early 1920s*

133

▲▼ *Two views of Dryburgh Abbey*

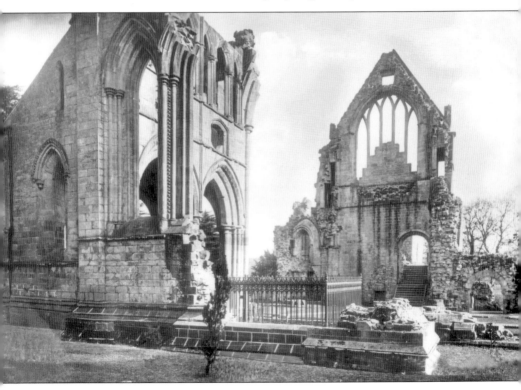

*Views of
Dryburgh Abbey*

▲ *St Catherine's
Window*

▶

St Mary's Aisle

▲ *The Presbytery,
at the East End
of the Abbey*

▶

*Dryburgh
Abbey
Cloisters*

▲ *Bemersyde House, the seat of the chief of Clan Haig*

▼ *The resting place of the 1st Earl Haig, Dryburgh Abbey*

▲ *Field-Marshal the 1st Earl Haig inset into a view of his grave, Dryburgh*

▼ *View of the Tweed and Eildons from Dryburgh*

The Orchard Gates, Dryburgh, with the Tweed and Eildons beyond

Earlston, Lauder, Thirlestane, Drygrange and Leaderfoot

▲ *Leaderfoot Bridge*   ▼ *Leaderfoot viaduct with Black Hill in background*

▲ *Carolside Bridge over Leader Water, Earlston*

◄

War Memorial, Earlston

◥

Rhymers Tower, Earlston

▶

Earlston Village

▲▼ *Two views of Kidgate, Earlston*

▲ *Church Street, Earlston*   ▼ *Station Road, Earlston*

▲ *Drygrange*　　　　　▼ *Drygrange and Leader Water*

▲ *The meeting of Leader Water with the River Tweed at Lauder*

▼ *Chesters Farm, East Lauder*

▼ *Spottiswoode Eagle Lodge, Lauder*   ▲ *Thirlestane Castle, Lauder*

◀ *Spottiswoode, Lauder*

Abbotsford, Melrose, Darnick and Lowood

▲ *Abbotsford, Home of Sir Walter Scott*

◥
Abbotsford Ferry

▶
Waverley Hydro, Melrose

149

▼ ▲ *Two views of Darnick Tower*

◄ *Eildon Hills*

▲ *Melrose and Valley*   ▼ *Melrose Abbey*

▲▼ *Two views of Melrose Abbey*

153

▲▼ *Two views of Melrose Square*

154

▲*Fairydean, Melrose*

▼ *Melrose from Weir Hill*

155

▶

Tweed suspension bridge, Melrose

▲

▼ *Melrose from Gattonside*   *The Tweed at Lowood, Melrose*

▲ *The Tweed from Gattonside Road, Melrose*

▼ *Looking to Melrose from Newstead Scaurs*

▲ *The Eildons, Melrose and river Tweed*

▼ *The Trimontium stone at the site of the Roman Fort at Melrose*

Galashiels and Stow

▲ *Abbotsview, Galashiels* ▼ *Abbotsview Dining Hall*
◄ *Galashiels War Memorial*

▲ *Abbotsview Home, Galashiels*　　　　　　　▼ *Netherbarns, Galashiels*

▲ *Galafoot Bridge*   ▼ *The Eildons from Langlee, Galashiels*

163

Galashiels Cornmill Square ▲

▶
The War Memorial, Galashiels

▼ *Galashiels from Bruce's Hill*

◀ *Gala from the Reservoir*

165

▲ *Gala Mercat Cross and St Pauls*　　　▼ *Moonlight on Gala Mercat Cross*

166

▲ *Galashiels High Street*

▼ *Gala Park, Scott Street*

▲ *Gala Braw Lads' Day, 1940s*

▶

Hillslap Tower, Glendearg, Galashiels

▲ *Stow pack horse bridge*　　　　　　　　　　　　　　　　▼ *Lugate Water, Stow*

▲ *Lugate Bridge, Stow*　　　　　　　　　　　▼ *Stow*

▲ *Stow Hotel*

▼ *Torsonce, Stow*

▲ *Stow from Lauder Road*　　　　　▼ *Bishop's Palace, Stow*

Peebles and the Tweed Valley

Tweed Valley from Caddonfoot

▲ *Ashiesteel from The Bridge*   ▼ *Shepherding near Ashiesteel*

▲ Ashiesteel House, Home of Sir Walter Scott from 1804-1812

▼ Clovenfords from the south

▲ *Elibank Tower*   ▼ *Elibank, Walkerburn*

▲ *Walkerburn from Flora Hill*   ▼ *Walkerburn West*

178

St Ronan's Wells

Innerleithen from west

▲▼ *Two views of Innerleithen High Street*

▲ *Innerleithen Station 1930s*   ▼ *Innerleithen and Tweed Valley*

◀ *Satyr Sykes, Traquair back road*   ▲ *Traquair Gates*

◣ *Traquair Kirk*   ▼ *Glentress, Leithen Water*

▼ ◀ ▲ *Three views of Glen House*

▼ *Peebles Barns Youth Hostel*　　　▲ *Peebles by the river Tweed*

◀ *Peebles Cauld*

187

▲ *Tweed Bridge, Peebles*   ▼ *A view of Peebles from the golf course*

◄ *Two views of Peebles High Street, from era of horse and cart to automobile*

189

▲◣ *Two views of Neidpath Castle*

▶

Tweedsmuir from reservoir

Ashkirk, Hawick, Minto and Langholm

▼ *Ashkirk* ▲▼ *Two views of Burnfoot from Weensland, 1958*

◣ *The Woll at Ashkirk*

◀ *Denholm Dean* ▲ *Denholm Green, Leyden Monument and United Reformed Church*

▼ *Weens, Bonchester Bridge*

▲▼ *Hawick postcards: Branxholme Tower and Lodge House*

▲ *Postcard of Hawick High Street* ▼ *Laurie Bridge, Hawick, c1949*

◀ *Harden, Hawick*　　　　　　　▲ *Hawick from Wilton Dean*

▼ *Hawick from Millars Knowes*

◀ *Hawick High Street*   ▲ *The 'Horse' 1514 memorial and Bridge Street, Hawick*

▼ *Putting and Bowls at Wilton Lodge Park*

▲ *Borthwick Water, with Goldielands Tower in the background*

▶
Three Trees corner, Mosspaul

▼ *The Old Coach Road, Hawick*

◀ *The Meeting of River Teviot and Borthwick Water, Hawick*

▲▼ *Two views of Minto Church*

▲ *Stobs Castle and Bridge, Hawick*   ▼ *Teviot view from Crumhaugh*

▲ *Branxholme Tower, Hawick, c.1949*   ▼ *Branxholme Tower*

▲ *Mosspaul* ▼ *Langholm, Gates of Eden*

207

▲ *Langholm, herding sheep over the River Esk*

▼ *Langholm meeting of Ewes Water and the River Esk*

Ancrum and Jedburgh

▲ *Ancrum Bridge end*

▼ *Ancrum*

▲ *Jeburgh Abbey and War Memorial*   ▼▶ *Two views of Jedburgh Abbey*

▲ *Jedburgh Abbey from church*   ▼ *Jedburgh Castle*

▲ *Jedburgh Auld Bridge*

▼ *Ferniehurst, ancient seat of the clan Kerr, was a Youth Hostel from 1934-1984*

▲ *Jedburgh from Allerley Well Park*   ▼ *Jedburgh from castle*

▲ *Hownam from steeple, Jedburgh*　　　　▼ *Jedburgh from Hartrigge*

215

◄▲
Queen Mary's House, Jedburgh

216

Kelso and Yetholm

▲▶
*Floors Castle,
Kelso*

▲ *The Teviot and the Tweed rivers meet at Kelso*   ▼ *Kelso from Teviot Bridge*

▲ *Kelso and the Tweed at dusk*   ▼ *Kelso bridge and Abbey*

▲ *Kelso Abbey* ▼ *Kelso town and Abbey*

▲ *Kelso High School*

▼ *The coronation of the Gypsy King at Kirk Yetholm, 1898*

▲ *Stitchill Lyn near Kelso*   ▼ *Yetholm Toll and Staerough*

▲ *Town Yetholm*   ▼ *Yetholm village*

▼ *Town Yetholm*   ▲ *Kirk Yetholm*

◄ *Kirk Yetholm from Cherrytrees*

Berwick, Eyemouth, and Coldingham

◀ *High Street, Berwick-on-Tweed*　　　▲ *Berwick-on-Tweed, early morning*

◣ *Castlegate, Berwick-on-Tweed*　　　▼ *Railway Bridge, Berwick-on-Tweed*

▲ *Eyemouth Fort and Bay*   ▼ *Rough seas at Eyemouth*

▲ *Eyemouth Bowling Club*   ▼ *Fishers Brae, Coldingham*

▲ *Burnside, Coldingham*　　　　　　　▼ *Coldingham Bay*

Borderers

Wat Barrie of Sundhope, Yarrow, who wrote for The Southern Reporter under the nom-de-plume of Henry J Clayboddie

▲*Charles Fa Blyth, Gypsy King, Kirk Yetholm*

◀

James Hislop,
aka, Jamsie the Tooph,
Selkirk

▶

A studio portrait
of a young
Marion Finlay,
née Watson

◄
Lady on a bicycle

►
*Friends and family
summer outing*

▼*Day trippers
at the
Grey Mare's Tail*

236

▲ *Burgh schoolboys, with Mr Millar and Mr Lusk*

▼ *Under Burgh School, Selkirk, 1884, 1st Standard with teachers*
Mr Millar and Miss Douglas

◄ *Upper Burgh School, Selkirk, 1888, 5th Standard with headmaster*
Mr James Millar and Assistant Mr James Aitken

Edwards Family Photographs

▲ *Nell Edwards*

▼▶ *Robert, John and Nell Edwards*

▼ *Robert Edwards*

▲ *The Edwards family and friends enjoying a picnic at the Ettrick Shepherd's Monument, St Mary's Loch following the annual open-air 'Blanket Preaching' service, 1887. It shows a young Robert Edwards lounging on the grass, far right*

▲ *Granny Plant,
mother of Jane Plant
and mother-in-law of
Andrew Edwards*

◤ *A portrait of Jane
Plant, wife of Andrew,
taken in the
A R Edwards
Photography Studio,
Tower Street, Selkirk*

▶

*Thomas Colledge,
Assistant to Andrew
Edwards photographed
the family of A R
Edwards following his
sudden death in 1891,
at just 42 years of age.
Standing – John and
Robert; seated, Agnes,
Jane (mother) and Nell*

240

▲◥ *Studio portraits of a young Robert*

▶ *Robert, middle left, with friends*

▼ *Pencil portrait of a girl by an 18 year-old Robert in 1897*

▲ Bob Edwards
with car and dog

◀ Robert and Peggy
on their Wedding
Day

▶

Peggy on her
Wedding Day

▶

Robert and Peggy
with their family,
Bessie, Bert and Jack

242

◀▶
Bessie Edwards as a baby and toddler

▼
The three siblings, Jack, Bert and Bessie

◀ *Bessie and Jack Edwards*

▼ *Bessie with friends, the Colledge sisters, Jean and Peggy*

◀
Bessie Edwards and soldier companion on a summer outing in her father's car

▼
Jack and Bessie, 1940

▲
Brothers Jack and Bert, with their father Robert and sister Bessie, 1940

▶
Bowls Pairs Winners, 1961 Championship, J. Brown and Robert Edwards (far right)

Family down under – Robert Edwards' sister and brother, Agnes and John, settled in Australia in the first half of the 20th century.

◀ Mrs Agnes Easton (née Edwards) on her wedding day 19ᵗʰ August 1939, Australia

▼ John Edwards (standing) photographed with friends in Australia

▲ John Edwards pictured at 29 years old in 1936 in Australia

◀ *Robert Edwards in profile*

▶ *Bessie Chick née Edwards*

▶

*Bessie Chick
in later years*

▼ *Pictured at a
Selkirk exhibition
of R. Clapperton
photographic archives
are (l to r) Liz Mack,
Margaret Edwards
and Cathy Chick,
all granddaughters
of Robert. Margaret
Edwards' father was
Bert, Bessie Chick's
brother*

◀

Cathy Chick with a display of her grandfather's cameras and photographic equipment at Selkirk Museum

▶

(l to r) • Magazine and plate camera with rack and pinion bellows . 'Challenge ' model, British made,(possibly) Lizars. Lens and mechanisim by Bausch and Lomb Optical company. Patent Jan 6th 1891. Original cost £3.00

• Kodak Folding Bellows Pocket Camera No. 3A model B5. Made 1900s by Eastman Kodak Company, Rochester, New York USA. Took roll film, each exposure close to half plate size.

• The 'Baroness' Camera (also pictured right, with plate holder and lens case): mahogany and brass body; lens by Steinheil of Munchin, Patent no. 23611 with waterhouse stop. Made by Houghton Butcher Manufacturing Co. Ltd., later known as 'Ensign' company. Supplied by James More, practical optician and photographic dealer, Glasgow.

▲ *Folding bellows pocket cameras (l to r)*

• *Ensign folding camera with Trichro shutter.*

• *Zeiss Ikon Ikonta Derval lens folding roll film camera*

• *Kodak Folding Bellows Pocket Camera No. 3A model B5. Made 1900s by Eastman Kodak Company*

• *Voigtlander Anastigmat Braunshcweig folding bellows film camera 1:7.7*

◀▲ *Further views of the 'Baroness' Camera, with (above) glass plate holder and interchangeable aperture plates*

Acknowledgements

The Selkirk Regeneration Company would like to thank the following for the parts they played in producing this book:

- Cathy Chick, Andrew Robert Edward's (ARE) great-granddaughter, for preserving and contributing the bulk of the archive.

- Margaret Edwards, ARE's granddaughter and Bessie Chick's niece for helping to fulfil Bessie's wish to publish a book on the Family Business of A R Edwards and Son.

- Liz Mack, ARE's other great-granddaughter and Bill Campbell for Family History details. David and Jo Edwards for family research.

- Janis Cornwall for laborious restoration, preparation of the photographs and planning the layout of the book

- Linda Cornwall, Scottish Borders Council, for her help with the Community Grant application which enabled us to publish this book.

The following individuals, mainly from Selkirk and surroundings, for their help and advice in the book's preparation:

- Janet Mitchell (Clapperton Studio archives)

- Jeremy Moncur, David Hislop, Gracie Bell and Allan Scott for contributing Edwards photographs from their own collections.

- Mr.and Mrs.G.Scott for rescuing negatives and gifting them to the archive.

- Richard Wood of Inverness for sharing his A R Edwards and Son Postcard collection.

- Penny McDonald for her help in proof reading.
- Dave Ayley for his tireless journeys with various Edwards Artefacts.
- Shona Sinclair and Zilla Oddy Hawick Museums Curators.
- Paul Brough and Morag Cockburn, Live Borders at Hawick Hub.
- Phoebe Stewart and Laura Debeate, Selkirk Museums Trust/ Museums Live
- Elma Fleming, Borders Family History Society. Research on the business history.
- Rachel May and Ted, Smail's Printworks Innerleithen, for details of Mr T Colledge who was locum Photographer after ARE's death.
- And finally, Scottish Borders Council's support in preserving this important Border's archive for posterity.

L. D. Neil